Psychic

Book One

Commander Collins's Will

memoir

Jacqueline   Lunger

Title: Commander Collins's Will
memoir

Book 1 Psychic Chronicles Series

Author: Jacqueline Lunger

Publisher: Ageless Knowledge

Hubert, North Carolina USA

Copyright December 2015

ISBN: 978-0-9747768-4-2

Table of Contents

Dedication:

To Life in all forms and planes of existence. Keep reminding us that we are eternal and constant.

"We are the sun, all other appearances are illusion." - 2015

Foreword:
by Reverend Todd Jay Leonard

The old adage "truth is stranger than fiction" certainly holds true for this riveting story about a mother's quest to fulfill a long-term companion's last wishes regarding his estate; the sketchy people selected to administer it; and her most important reason for seeking justice—her son's rightful inheritance from his father. Her personal motivation to look out for her son's best interests would have been sufficient reason for most people to fight for what is right, but she had an additional, otherworldly justification for pursuing, with a vengeance, the truth—Commander Collins, her longtime companion, reached out to her from the other side of the veil to ensure his dying wishes were fulfilled, and that their son Chris' inheritance was properly administered. Commander Collins's unwavering and consistent clairvoyant assistance allowed Jacqueline to unravel a very complicated legal dispute regarding his estate and future trust for their son.

In Commander Collins's Will, Jacqueline Lunger artfully crafts a narrative from her own life into a story which is part mystery, part romance, and part metaphysical in a fight for righteousness. A developed and certified Spiritualist medium, she relied on her psychic and mediumistic gifts to get to the bottom of a dilemma that was not only personal and very human, but one that involved Spirit and spirituality. She begins an arduous journey of doing what is right which also had an added advantage of erasing any karmic debt that involved associations from past lives possibly related not only to her family, estate lawyers, executors, and public officials but also the long process allowed her to experience more deeply her own, personal spiritual growth as a medium and psychic.

Not all psychics are mediums, but all mediums are certainly psychic. It can be quite tricky to balance the two gifts, but the ability to access both can also be quite enriching and beneficial to those on the earth plane…and to those in Spirit seeking contact with loved ones here through a medium. This book describes the struggle of such a medium who is also psychic. More importantly, however, it is a story about a mother whose love for her son is so strong that nothing can stop her from pursuing truth and justice. In the process, she receives many valuable lessons in life and spirit—not only learning about the complicated legal system that she was forced to maneuver through, but also learning about her own spirituality and karma; getting in touch more deeply with her own intuitive gifts; and learning how to listen clairaudiently in order to decipher the messages that are contained in spirit communication.

Commander Collins's Will

Psychic Chronicles Series, Book 1

Jacqueline Lunger author

Prologue:

Jacqueline Lunger is the author and psychic medium Commander Collins enlisted to help defend his Last Will and Testament following the massive heart attack that soundly and unexpectedly delivered him into the Spirit world one December morning in 1983. Jacqueline writes about factual psychic-mediumship encounters in order to give voice to those who have lost their own and help the reader gain understanding of what the process of spirit communication is like. She draws attention to the difference between her own psychic senses informing her and Commander Collins's other consciousness directions. Jacqueline also presents the reader with a unique point of view regarding the afterlife and demonstrates why other worldly encounters can be beneficial.

In this nonfiction work, a true account of actual events, she describes people and circumstances surrounding the Last Will and Testament of Commander Earl C. Collins, USN-R, and the communications and guidance he provided to her in an effort to restore the plans he had so carefully written down. Jacqueline makes the comparison of her journey and growth through these experiences to that of Prince Arjuna in the **Bhagavad Gita,** an ancient Hindu Holy Book, sometimes referred to as *The Gita*. The story attempts to illustrate causes for a justified war engaging an ethical warrior.

When Westerners can't make a deal to resolve an issue of power and control we soon go to war and do our best to win. In ancient Eastern culture, the identical situation might bring consequences for generations. Accepting that negative karma is a possibility of decisions and actions adds a layer of consideration that might bring creative solutions before resorting to war.

The author finds herself in a situation much like Prince Arjuna after Commander Collins crosses into the world of Spirit. She is immediately faced with a hostile interloper. She searches her conscience and prays for divine guidance. Jacqueline is an experienced psychic medium who is mindful of the interconnectedness of life. She believes people are sharing the same life force, challenges and opportunities. This understanding causes her to reach for a higher perspective in times of stress and serious decision making. She finally accepts that she is the only person who can provide Commander Collins the help he requires. Intuition and psychic images and messages encourage her to take up the challenge presented and manage the situation. Jacqueline moves forward on shaky legs traversing uncharted terrain. Did she have the courage to carry out the years of challenging tasks that were coming? Would the Commander be there to guide her through all the snares and landmines she was foreseeing? What motivated her to stick with the arduous journey she found herself immersed in? You will have to read the story to find the answers to those and other question arising throughout the story.

Chapter I: Shaken Awake

The year 1983 brought me into a series of important unexpected legal situations accompanied by psychic perceptions and guidance from the other side of life. These collective experiences changed the big picture of my understanding of life forever more. I came to realize, in retrospect, that this was my personal *trial by fire*, or my *Gita* as Eastern philosophies might say. I am now able to look back on the matter with 32-years of hindsight. No one who is aware of my experiences will be able to say my life has had no purpose or that it was boring. Now at age 64, I can honestly say I bless it all and give thanks for each person, place and event I've shared this lifetime with. Boring it has not been!

A lifetime of psychic experiences taken for granted and usually employed for social and entertainment purposes were in fact preparing me for the serious work that would require all of my skills and abilities. Every experience served to lead me to this current challenge. Suddenly my peculiar abilities were essential; necessary, and important. Intuition brought information and a perspective that I couldn't have reached merely through logical thinking. My mediumship skills helped me to make strong connections with Commander Collins that provided a clear channel for his valuable guidance to pour through.

Realizing my previous encounters in the paranormal and metaphysical arena were all preparing me for these more serious legal matters, I embraced and honored my psychic senses as precious tools with vital and practical uses. I already knew people were assisted by those in the spiritual planes and that the perspective they bring to us is much wiser and more complete than our own. I accepted that I had been tapped to use my psychic skills for a positive outcome even though I recognized I was walking into some dark and treacherous waters, thanks to those with less honorable, self-serving motives. I am still human and experience all the same human thoughts and feelings as others do. I thought of the opposition as greedy, bottom feeding bastards more than once. Having that thought served to remind me of the importance of seeing these matters through to the end.

Psychic readings during my teenage years had often been enjoyable and entertaining. I had experienced paranormal occurrences since early childhood. I knew what it was like to sit aloft and commune with the heavens, and it certainly didn't take chemical stimulation to get me there. My youthful experiences were preparation for the mature entryway that 1983 ushered in. Accepting my psychic mediumship work as a calling has allowed me to be rewarded with a unique and worthwhile career. I trust you will enjoy reading each chapter, as I share my real life experiences connected to Commander Collins's Will.

Retired Navy Commander Earl Collins was 58 when he suffered a fatal heart attack one December morning in 1983. He was dressing to go to his law office as he did each day when the heart attack instantly took him to Summerland, the Spiritualist term for Heaven or the afterlife. His body was found beside his closet by a workman. He was surrounded by his loyal Weimaraners, Katie and Heidi.

Services were promptly arranged for a military funeral, as he had served in the Navy for twenty-three years before retiring in Jacksonville, North

Carolina. Earl remains to this day a very dear friend, mentor, and much loved co-parent of my son, Chris.

Earl's casket was barely in the ground—the sun had not set yet—when the challenge over the management of his estate entered my home, confronting me with a need to make rapid choices for which I had not been prepared. His Will named an executor and an alternate. The alternate must have followed me home from the service. He quickly paid me an unexpected visit saying he was angry because he had not been given the executor's job. He didn't hesitate to tell me that he thought Earl had overlooked him on this count and he felt cheated on a commercial property they had jointly invested in, as well. I knew Earl could be shrewd and crafty but he didn't foul his own nest. The commercial building he referred to was an office building they each operated their businesses out of. I sensed that his plan was to intimidate me into supporting an attack on the named executor. Clearly he didn't know me. Intimidation just doesn't win me over. When faced with no alternative but fight or flight, I normally fight. There is an indignant feeling that rises up in me and it takes over if I allow it. I informed him that I needed a day or two to think things over and I would get back to him.

I was weathering a storm of feelings: immense sadness, confusion, insecurity, fear, unpreparedness, and the sense of being totally overwhelmed with the range of tasks and challenges I could now foresee. I had goose bumps when Matt, the challenger, uttered the name of an out of town lawyer, Ed Spencer. I didn't know this new lawyer but I knew psychically that he was behind Matt's plan to launch a formal attack over the management of Earl's Will. Not only did hearing his name give me goosebumps but I had a tightness in the stomach that was a sign of negative events to come. I'd heard through the grapevine that Ed Spencer had moved into our area from another state to be near his grandchildren. His son-in-law was a well thought of local attorney.

Earl had explained his intentions regarding his estate to me several times over our years together. We had not married; however, he did adopt my young son from a previous marriage. We lived together as a family for many years. We shared parenting and our son's future mattered a great deal to both of us. Chris had turned twelve just ten days before Earl's passing. Chris greatly admired his dad. My son was devastated by his father's passing. Earl Collins was a unique person with a brilliant mind and a great sense of humor. There is not another man like him on the planet. He would be greatly missed and fondly remembered by many, but by none more than his son.

I quickly faced a fear that I'd hidden so well during Matt's visit. My inner senses pressed upon me the seriousness of the path we were going to travel. I had to accept that the plan had morphed into a whole new field of concerns. Things had gone way off course. I was thirty-three years old and a single parent with a grieving child. I was still trying to rebalance myself and my own sense of loss. Knowing that our loved ones continue to live in other planes of life doesn't lessen our grief when they transition. We still grieve the loss of the physical person and our face to face interactions.

I worked as a business manager at a nearby medical clinic and had no legal education or experience. The ominous danger I saw approaching would require all of my best perceptions and abilities. I also knew that I would have everything I would need when the time came to engage. I had a larger and more complicated job now, but could I handle it? If I did nothing it would be disloyal; I would be abandoning my duty to Earl and our son. If I acted I might behave poorly, maybe even making things worse instead of better. I was quickly reminded of The Bhagavad Gita.

The Bhagavad Gita is a well-known holy Hindu book and it has been studied for centuries. In the *Gita*, Prince Arjuna sits in his chariot overwhelmed by grief. He feels incapable of making a decision about the future of his kingdom and the effect on his family. His decision would affect the whole kingdom. His beloved father, the king, has passed away. Arjuna's evil cousin brings a large army and sits on a ridge across the valley, threatening to take the crown and kingdom for himself. The Prince knows he must serve and protect his people as his father had prepared him to do. The thought of spilling his own family's blood is repulsive and unacceptable to him. Doing so would bring disgrace to his ancestors. In tremendous angst, Arjuna calls out for guidance to Lord Krishna, who then appears in his chariot. Lord Krishna informs Arjuna that he must fight his cousin. The would-be king asks, "Will I win if I do?" Krishna tells him the outcome of the battle isn't important. "You must fight. It is your dharma." Dharma is defined as one's path of righteousness or in accordance with Natural Law. Suddenly, my present situation had a context I could relate to and that gave me a sense of direction. I must fight and I must win. I must fight wisely!

If I truly fought to the best of my abilities and lost it would be Divine Will. If I fought and won, that too would be Divine Will. If I decided not to fight or to engage in battle lackadaisically I would have added to the negative karma that the situation appeared to have been caused by.

As the sole guardian of our twelve-year-old son, Chris, I couldn't ignore the need to be vigilant and prudent about assets from Earl's estate that were going to become his trust fund. Once the estate was settled and the inheritance taxes were paid, Chris was the sole beneficiary. The federal estate tax was much higher in 1983, unfortunately. Earl expected things to go smoothly; his plans were not complicated. I could see funds spewing out of the accounts with no good result. When an estate is legally challenged it must pay the costs of both sides of the dispute. What could I do? Sit by passively and allow a bully, or worse, to manage things, or try to pay enough attention to feel confident things were going the way Earl had wished?

I felt a moral responsibility to honor Earl's wishes. I felt a mother's need to defend my son's inheritance from the greedy bottom feeding bastards circling around now.

I would soon have a crash course on legal proceedings and lawyers. I never expected to want or need to know all that I learned during the next four years. It was an arduous time made more manageable by spirit communication and guidance from Infinite Intelligence, a term for higher consciousness wisdom. I tackled legal research making note and paying attention to details. I am usually not interested in details. The right outcome was my highest priority. Quickly, I outgrew my insecurities and learned to handle myself under fire. I was able to anticipate the adversary's next moves often enough to slow them down. The battles took several unexpected twists and turns but I was prepared for them each time. Earl was guiding me through their devious plots successfully.

The information and documents that I had to obtain were easily revealed to me. Some of it even came from psychic sources. I found myself repeatedly led to the right person or place to ask for and get what I needed. I didn't know why they might possess something helpful, but I believed they had some important information for me. I had to cast aside my awkwardness and ask directly for a meeting without being able to explain why I wanted to meet more than once.

The first of a series of such meetings was with Phil Payne the day after Earl's funeral. I didn't question why I needed to meet with Phil, I just knew that I did. Intuition works to inform, prepare and protect us if we will only learn to listen. *Knowing* that Phil Payne could assist me helped me to sleep well after Matt left my home. I trusted that Phil would agree to see me tomorrow and that the meeting would go well. It honestly went better than I'd expected it would. Phil was probably the only person in town who would have shared such vital and shocking news with me.

I explained the intended challenge to Earl's Will from Matt to displace the named executor. My first feeling was that Phil could help me because he and Matt were both in the insurance industry and likely knew each other. Phil listened carefully to everything I said. He paid attention. Like Prince Arjuna, I felt relieved just being taken seriously. Then Phil said, "I know something about the retired, out of town lawyer you mentioned, and you probably ought to be aware of it." The lawyer he referred to was stirring things up behind the scenes, prompting Matt, the substitute executor, to take action to overthrow the named executor. I'd had goose bumps just hearing his name the day before. After this meeting with Phil I had a clearer picture of him. He obviously saw the opportunity to take control of the estate for himself, through Matt, his new friend. Phil informed me that he knew from Ed's own mouth that he was being disbarred in another state for mismanaging trust funds of the insurance company he had worked for. I understood fully why this stranger was involved now. He was no friend of ours or Matt's. Matt was too dumb to see what he was trying to pull off. I understood that I had to act quickly in every way to destroy his plans.

Phil Payne provided me with everything I needed at that time during our visit. First, he confirmed that I was correct to seek important information from him, and then he told me why I had come there. He operated a popular insurance office in town. Phil knew where the bodies were buried. He kept current on local gossip and rumors. I was relieved to learn the information provided hadn't come from his rumor mill. I am grateful for the help he provided to us that day.

I left his office surprised, wide eyed, even amazed at the accuracy of spirit's precise guidance. I hadn't anticipated that Ed, the retired lawyer, would be anything more than a pestering nuisance looking for something to do. I asked Phil how he knew about the disbarment. He said, "Ed came to me when he moved to town and set out a plan for estate investments he planned to promote locally. I pulled down the statute book from the shelf, as he pointed to the shelf of books behind his chair. I showed him exactly where his proposal was forbidden by law in this state. That is when he informed me that his Ohio law license was inactive and why. Clearly he hadn't learned his lesson."

Now I was on full alert, there was more than just an estate management problem here. Earl was accessing my psychic senses, and had pinpointed a dangerous character right from day one. I am so glad I paid attention to the knowing I had and followed through on it. The disreputable lawyer had his sights on Earl's estate. I.e. my son's inheritance. I knew I would put a stop to his plan, as soon I learned how to do it. My confidence increased, but just slightly.

I promptly reported the results of both meetings I'd had since Earl's funeral to the primary executor, a thirty-something female attorney who had office space in Earl's building. She wasn't a partner, but I knew he had planned to groom her into one over time. She cautioned me against telling anyone what I'd learned. Phil's message was all the proof I needed and there was nothing to be gained by telling anyone else.

Chapter II: A Righteous Battle

I received a summons for a hearing about the estate the following day. My legal role was guardian of the minor person, who was also my son, Chris. I was, for all intents and purposes, his regent, empowered to make decisions and act on his behalf. I was able to act as his voice in all matters regarding the estate and the future trust. As far as the angry challenger, Matt, and his good friend, dishonest Ed, were concerned, I was the fly in the ointment that they needed to quickly scare into doing nothing. They had made another mistake, assuming I didn't understand my legal role in these matters. I was a named beneficiary and the mother and legal guardian of the primary benefactor. Being pleasant and easy going can mislead some people into discounting your intelligence, especially if you are female.

The summons I received showed that Matt had retained seven lawyers made up of several different firms in town. Did he think he could prevent me from having an attorney by monopolizing all the best ones? His plan just made me angrier and more determined to see that he failed. I would battle him and win, too! A famous American medium and healer, Edgar Cayce once said, "It's alright to be angry, just don't use it to sin".

"Greedy bottom feeding bastards" was my first thought about his dirty band of disloyal lawyers. How dare they try to gang up on me? Didn't they have any sense of loyalty to Earl? "No honor among thieves" rang in my mind. By then I'd learned that the estate was paying the cost of all actions and legal representatives for all sides engaged in this ridiculous sideshow of a hearing that shouldn't even be happening. I was again directed by Earl from spirit to make the most efficient response to the hearing's summons.

Earl guided me to retain an attorney from outside the local bar association. Why outside the local bar, I wondered? Earl answered my question mentally, "Local attorneys engage in compromises, wheeling and dealing with cases daily. You need someone who doesn't owe any of them anything and doesn't expect to encounter them again." I accepted his direction without further questions. I did not hear voices or see written signs. I trusted his mental message to be to our benefit.

The next day I met with an attorney in another county who agreed to obtain the resignations of the opposition and his seven lawyers. The hearing never even started, I am happy to report. Resignations were immediately obtained in the jury room while we were gathered in the courtroom. Thanking my attorney, I exhaled deeply, smiled brightly, and never saw her or the opposition players again. She performed well for us.

I did a little victory shuffle, raising my arms and shaking my head in celebration after the successful non-hearing. I truly believed all threats had been eliminated and the future would be straight ahead and level. I soon had to accept that this challenge was just one of several reasons for me to outmaneuver an assortment of greedy, self-serving opponents during the next few years.

A contractor employed by the appointed executor for remodeling work at the office building and the family home would become an expensive, long lasting point of combat. I reviewed and challenged his written contract before any work was started at either location. The executor had permitted him to write his own contracts for the jobs. I found that decision outrageous. She was an attorney trained in contracts this wasn't making any sense to me. The labor portion of his contracts were far too generous to be realistic in the local economy. I stated it was unacceptable and needed to be modified, providing examples that were more in keeping with similar work being done in town at that time. I mistakenly thought she had made the changes when she didn't disagree with me.

I learned that the contracts had not been amended a couple of years later. I was forced to bring up issues of negligence and mismanagement of trust funds before settling the estate and eventually replacing her.

My next hostile engagement was to challenge the buyout calculations and amount paid to Matt, Earl's real estate partner. This unpleasant matter came up soon after displacing him as the alternate executor.

I sought a clear mind and open heart to help to guide me along the mired and rocky path I covered. Meditations were like classroom lessons some days. Earl let me know that he was surprised by the reckless actions of people he had expected he could rely on to manage his estate and subsequent trust. He regretted trusting either of them adding that "you can only work with what you have at the time." I was able to provide him the opportunity to participate in making things better via my mediumship skills. We were a good team in this world and from the other side, too. Not that we always agreed on everything.

I honestly wondered if this earthly mess was keeping Earl from pursuing his own interests in the afterlife. He made it clear to me that this was his priority for now. After all, it was a mess of his creation that we were working to clean up.

Reimbursement of office utilities, taxes, repairs and cleaning fees for the office building were not to be refunded to the real estate partner. I pointed this out to the executor and repeated that message more than once. Matt had submitted a claim for every penny spent from the initial day he and Earl purchased the office building to the present time.

Matt and Earl had a written real estate partnership including a buy/sell condition. Matt said he had to sell; he could not afford to buy the building. He expressed resentment that there was no insurance to cover his purchase of the building. Matt was going around town saying Earl had screwed him out of the building. It's very rude to speak so ill of the deceased. Matt was in the insurance business. Why didn't he take care of that if it mattered to him?

I remember a particular moment of self-pity I experienced. I thought I might deserve some kind of combat ribbon for the battles I seemed to be regularly engaged in. I had an immediate spiritual reprimand that "lately I was the one doing all the shooting, and I was pretty good at it, too." Underdog no more, I decided to see myself as a capable winner!

Matt's itemized calculations were so inflated no one could have afforded to buy the building. He was entitled to his half of the cost of the building and paid remodeling expenses, performed to date, in my opinion. Or, he could receive half of the current appraised value of the building but nothing else seemed fair and reasonable to me. Earl affirmed my thinking. I didn't go to law school but I expected that anyone who had graduated from law school should have known and applied one of these common methods to negotiate a building buyout settlement.

I sensed intuitively that the executor was trying to avoid any more conflict with Matt. I learned what could be valid reasons for her to have that desire. Her husband was the pastor of a local church. Matt and the contractor were members of her husband's church. Matt and his wife had a good deal of influence with the churches' board of directors. Matt might have an influence on the executor's family, their income and her husband's job security. The greedy contractor also was a member of this same church, and sang in the choir.

It was easy to recognize the impact of these simultaneous challenges; the contractor was remodeling the executor's own home at the same time she contracted with him to work on the estate's commercial building and residential property. The real estate partner had influence over the executor's husband's job security and income. The executor had created a treacherous mess in her life, and mine, by hiring the contractor. Isn't it good practice to avoid overlapping interests? I think so. Obviously she wasn't guided psychically and didn't appear to think beyond the moment. I'm not sure what methods she employed for decision making but they didn't suit me.

This scenario and cast of characters looked like something William Shakespeare would have created rather than the result of actual unscripted people in real life. They were connected in several intertwined arenas. Their motives were all greedy and self-serving or self-protecting. My son, the primary beneficiary, only had me to fight for his rights and property. Scenarios can't get this intertwined in one lifetime. This was karma in action if there ever was such a thing!

A close friend pointed out, "Earl gave you a big job but no gun to do it with." The plot was dark, multi-layered, and twisted. Success relied on keeping a clear head, remaining open to intuitive promptings, and accepting guidance from Spirit, as well. Karmic situations make for good stories. My invisible gun was universal spiritual help guiding me through the overlapping plots and characters so that the best actions could offer everyone freedom from the karma.

I use the term "clear head" in the above statement because a good psychic cannot take his/her own knowledge, prejudice or personal feelings into account when receiving and understanding messages from beyond this plane of life. It must be as if you are a blank slate (clear), or the information can be tainted and misinterpreted. Holding a neutral position mentally takes courage and practice but failing to do so muddies the next steps and the messages.

I find it humorous when someone tries to judge a spiritual reader as "just a psychic" or "just a medium" when we are all using the same inner senses to receive information. It is an easy and natural step into mediumship, once a person is utilizing their psychic or inner senses comfortably. It requires faith, and being able to release the fear of being wrong or ridiculed. Intentions to be of faithful and sincere service provide the golden key to connect with those who have the ability to help us from a higher plane or vibration.

Where do messages come from? A variety of answers are correct. Messages can be received by our own psychic ability to perceive and interpret energy employing our inner senses. They can also be directed from the other side of life, often called the astral plane, by loved ones and from spiritual beings or entities in higher planes.

A few months after Earl's passing, Chris and I moved into his house with my two dogs and Earl's three, making them five in all. I experienced an early morning visit while I was putting laundry away just prior to leaving for work soon after we moved in. I recognized that it was Earl. I was wide-eyed, not expecting his visit at that time. The event was immediately confirmed by Earl's dog, Katie.

I walked into the bedroom, with clean clothes in my arms and the dog following me, as Katie always did. I sensed a warm loving energy in the room. It seemed familiar. I was waiting for more information to identify its source. I noticed the warm comfortable energy was coming into the bedroom on the rays of sunlight streaming in the window. It became more concentrated as I focused on the spot in the room where it was focused. It was Earl. I recognized him with certainty, and so did Katie. She had her ears up. She was standing high on her toes as if she was ready to jump up, and she was wagging her tail. She was focused on the same area of the room that I felt his energy gather. We were both very happy to be with him again. After basking in his loving energy and mentally sending loving messages to him, I walked out of the room with Katie in tow, curious to see what would happen next.

I returned to the laundry room and carried Chris's clothes into his room. He was still asleep. School was out for the summer and there was nothing pressing, so no need to wake him early. The exact experience that occurred in my room was repeated again in his. Katie was reacting just as she had earlier. I knew for sure that Earl had an important reason for visiting us. I was clueless as to what it might be. I was too close to Earl to trust myself to sort out his reason to visit; my feelings could get in the way. We were still grieving. I looked for help from a well-known non-profit paranormal agency. I began my search by recalling my knowledge of J. B. Rhine's research program at Duke University from years earlier.

You probably won't be surprised to learn that I spent my high school time reading about Rhine's research with ESP, Carl Jung's affirming work on intuition and Spiritual reality, as well as Edgar Cayce's trance work for psychic guidance and physical healing. I was the student in the back of the classroom reading a book that interested me tucked inside the assigned textbook. I wasn't wasting time; I was learning something more interesting.

Chapter III: Meet the Mediums

I began my search for a quality medium by calling the Parapsychology Department at Duke University. A self-identified spoon bender answered the phone. That didn't impress me and I wondered if I'd called a wrong number. Spoon bending is a type of physical energy manipulation. It's a harsh energy to sensitives and people either like it or they don't. Young people usually enjoy playing with it. I haven't met anyone who didn't have one opinion or the other about spoon bending.

The guy from Duke Parapsychology put me in touch with Dr. William Roll. Dr. Roll had been Dr. Rhine's research assistant at Duke previously. It is said that Dr. Rhine brought enough money into the

47

university that Duke was happy to provide him research space. Once he passed into spirit, they didn't expect Dr. Roll would be able to maintain the benefactors so they decided to end the program.

Dr. Roll was now located near Duke, but was no longer a part of the university. When I contacted Dr. Roll's non-profit research agency I was informed that he only investigated physical phenomena. Earl's visits didn't qualify as physical phenomena. I didn't have rapping or tapping, no objects moved on their own, nor sounds, fires, etc. to report. Dr. William Roll is best known for the book, *Poltergeist*. His research and book are nothing like the popular movie of the same name.

The man I spoke with at Dr. Roll's nonprofit agency informed me that there were agency volunteers who occasionally did private work out in the field. I asked him to pass my name and phone number on to a good one. I have nothing against students; some do excellent work. Everyone begins as a student in all fields of work. I was sure someone would call me soon.

I received a call from one of the volunteers who was interested in coming to my home within a few minutes of hanging up the phone. Shane was located in Durham, about a 3 hour drive from me. She added that she was a high school English teacher. She reported that she had a strong interest and lots of experience in Spirit communication. We set an appointment and she added that she would likely bring a second medium with her.

Our appointment was scheduled to take place 4 days later. Right at 2:30 pm, my doorbell rang and I experienced colored lights flashing before me as I approached the door. I was having unprompted, open-eyed clairvoyance, a rare experience. I sensed the lights' message as "pay attention, pay close attention." I wondered if the visitors would think I was weird, or if I would think they were weird? There was a lot going on as I reached for the doorknob. I am pleased to report that we found each other agreeable and quite sane.

We soon sat in my bedroom where Earl's initial visitation had occurred. Our chairs were in a circle. Sunlight came through the windows. Earl came in energetically, immediately showing himself to each of us by sitting at a desk and looking at ledger pages. He was slapping the desk, saying "damn, damn, damn." I accepted the image as a message that he was upset about the estate's expenses. Not surprising, at all.

We walked outside the house and got into the boat at the river's edge. We visited Earl's island, a short distance down the river. I know it's unusual to own an island, but he did. He was always looking for a good deal on things and the island was no exception. He purchased one half of it from one person, and later the other half from the person's partner saying they were unable to get anyone to purchase it. Earl wasn't wasteful. It was very easy to understand his reaction to the way his resources were being handled.

I knew intuitively when preparing for our meeting that we were going on the boat. I didn't know why, but I made sure it was gassed up and ready to go. I didn't know even after we reached the island why we were there. The male medium steered the boat; his body language and handling of the vessels were so much like Earl's that I had to comment on it. I had not told the visiting mediums of the island's existence but one of them knew there was a place up the river and said we needed to go there.

It seemed to me that Earl was speaking through them in code, as if there was a secret he didn't want exposed. I was puzzled; I didn't know what to make of it. I learned directly from him, he was mentally telling me, that he didn't want them to know the extent of his assets. There weren't many sizable estates in southeastern North Carolina and he didn't want his business broadcasted. That thinking was just like him. It served as another confirmation of the connection made today.

David, the male medium asked if he could visit the storage room in the carport when we returned to the house. I took him to the storage room, and he began reaching into a cardboard box pulling out building plans. He asked if the activity made sense to me. I told him that Earl had talked about building a cottage on the island that we'd just returned from visiting. He asked if there were any building projects going on now or in the recent past. Yes, of course, the office building and the home had been remodeled since his passing. I knew suddenly, the contractor's expenses had to be investigated invoice by invoice.

Spirit's messages that were received that day were accurate, helpful, and caused me to want to learn more about the style of mediumship I'd observed today. I wanted to become more consistent in my own work with Spirit.

One of the mediums asked if Earl had a preferred religion. Earl was raised Methodist and he used to say he believed in the God of IBM. He meant that he believed we were evaluated by how well we used the gifts and talents God gave us. Imagine a giant computer in the sky keeping track of our endeavors. According to him, once we get into the after world, God will push the total key. The number a person ends up with determines whether or not we get into heaven. The mediums broke up laughing hysterically when I shared Earl's understanding of religion. They had way too much laughter; it meant they shared an inside joke. I learned that David was employed at IBM as a software engineer, once they could talk again. Spirit loves a good laugh, too.

I probed the mediums about the training they had received as they were preparing to leave. They said that they both studied with Patricia Hays at The Arthur Ford Academy of Mediumship. It was located in Spring Lake, NC when they were students there. I learned that the school recently relocated to a suburb of Atlanta, Georgia. They suggested I contact Patricia about joining a class soon. We had worked well together. I knew I would see them again.

I hadn't kept this meeting a secret. In fact I told the executor that it was scheduled and invited her and the clerk from the court to attend. She declined adding that her husband was interested and might come by. He didn't show up or call to cancel.

Chapter IV: In the Combat Zone

Back in the combat zone, I learned, after a little probing into the estate's bills, that there had been no organized record keeping of the contractor's expenses. The executor just paid the bills without question or comparison whenever he submitted one. Clearly the executor was inept at the very least; maybe even lazy, or possibly just not interested in doing a good job? Or perhaps she was getting some other benefit, a kickback or a big discount on her own construction work? Maybe this or maybe that, but it didn't really matter. I didn't know what was wrong with her or care why she wasn't doing her job. The explanations were of no use or value.

I was just tired of fighting everything all the time, one battle and then another. I resented being bothered by it, yet again. The need to fight another big issue was outrageous and it still fell to me to see that it was done. I was shaking my head and silently screaming "NO! NO! NO!" All the while, I was asking for guidance from a wiser and calmer source at the same time. Here was another battle, inside of me—the human woman and the spiritual woman—both were learning to accommodate each other and to coexist under pressure.

What I was experiencing must be similar to adrenal exhaustion. I was having difficulty bouncing back to my usual energy level. I silently questioned if I'd messed up running the alternate guy off in the beginning. My inner voice spoke right up," No, that was the right thing to do for sure!" He was the puppet of a professional thief, based on what I'd learned. I didn't know why Earl's estate was taking the hairpin turns it was, but it had to end, and soon. Combat gear is heavy. I was fatigued for sure. I wanted to get on with my life and didn't feel able to do so until this estate and trust were on secure ground. Looking back thirty-three years later, I was blessed to be able to learn so much about myself so quickly through these matters.

In February 1986, I attended a week long intensive at The Arthur Ford

Academy of Mediumship. Patricia Hays calls that week "boot camp." It's a prerequisite to her more in-depth programs. Through fortunate turns of events, thank you Spirit and Earl, I had the support I needed to be able to travel to Atlanta. Our good friends, Lee and Al were building a new home. The one they were selling sold so fast they had to find an interim place to stay for several months. I invited them to live with us while they built their new home. I needed someone to help with my son so that I could travel to Georgia for the class. Chris already considered them his family so it was a convenient and easy arrangement for all of us.

Lee's dad, Chet, moved in too; he was the contractor, overseer, plumber and chief cook. Chet was a unique character who grew up in Boston with Polish parents and much older sisters. He was a multi talented man with a big heart and a Boston accent that erupted in a booming voice. He didn't hesitate to show you all he knew and explain why things were the way they were. He and Chris became buddies. As much as Chris objected to Chet bossing him around, he enjoyed his company. Chris loved going to businesses with Chet and he would come home with hilarious stories of what Chet said, or did, that no one in the world would have said or done.

Just to provide an example, Chris came home one morning after being out with Chet. He was cracking up about something that happened at Arby's. Apparently Chet was used to having his breakfast at McDonalds and because he was a senior citizen he received his coffee for free there. He placed his order at Arby's adding that he wanted the free senior coffee, as well. When the cashier told him they didn't have free coffee, he loudly said, "Then cancel the order I'm going to McDonalds." Upon hearing that announcement the manager rushed to the counter and gave him the free coffee.

Chapter V.   Fight Like a Girl

My week at The Arthur Ford International Academy of Mediumship was exactly the restful, restorative and rejuvenating experience that I needed. Patricia Hayes, her staff, and I clicked immediately. She chuckled when she told me I had almost waited too long to connect with her. Her class was fun and playful for me. I considered it a refresher course and a getting to know you period. I loved each person and every activity we did together. Well, maybe not spoon bending, *snicker*. Physical psychic activities require harsher kinetic energy that most sensitive people would rather avoid. I did learn how to be more consistent in my reading connections and her lecture on psychic ethics was most welcome.

I learned that Patricia used to work for Arthur Ford in Florida before his transition following a massive heart attack. Arthur Ford is still one of America's most famous mediums. He had been a protestant minister serving in the US Army as a chaplain in Europe during World War I. He described in his autobiography, how he began to dream the casualty list the day before he received the written paper list. He also began to notice an unusual glow about the heads of the men listed prior to them going into battle.

When the war ended, Arthur traveled to India to study mysticism. Nothing in his Christian education could explain his experiences. The experiences he could not deny having caused his curiosity to dominate his life. Curiosity led him to travel the globe networking with others who were experimenting and researching in the metaphysical-paranormal field. His contacts included Sir Arthur Conan Doyle and most of Europe's prominent psychics of the day. I have read all of his books. Pick them up if you come across one because most are out of print now. I recently received one that he had autographed.

Dr. William Roll and Patricia collaborated on some investigations while she was in North Carolina. After she moved to Georgia, Dr. Roll relocated nearby and taught graduate classes at Georgia University. I met him several times because some of his graduate students were participating in an experimental healing method Patricia channeled from Spirit, called RoHun Therapy.

Meanwhile, back in North Carolina, I was able to retain original invoices of materials and actual labor cost records that the contractor had been paid for. I had the proof I needed to make a strong case for the executor's failure to perform the duties of her office prudently. I learned that the law requires each action of a fiduciary must pass the "prudent man rule." It means that you do not use resources managed for others as if they were your own, but that you consider what a prudent person would likely do when making decisions. No question about it, she failed the prudent man rule repeatedly.

I recalled hearing the contractor brag one day early in our dealings that everyone who worked on his jobs was licensed and insured. I was prompted by Earl to check him out with the State Contractors' Office. I discovered he was not licensed and unable to acquire insurance without a license. I know it's incredulous, but the executor continued to employ him even after I proved that he wasn't licensed or insured. He performed construction at her home and her mother's home. I barred him from our property. I questioned what could possibly hijack her judgment? I decided it wasn't worth thinking about and my responsibilities were the same regardless of her reasons.

The executor's mother's move to town had been foretold to me during a meditation about four months before she actually relocated. When preparing to go into meditation, I had asked the question, "When will all the estate conflict be over?" I received this response: "When her mother gets involved." The answer made no sense at the time. Her mother had visited a few times but lived several states away. I didn't know of any plans for her to move closer.

I accepted the end was close at hand, when I learned her mother was relocating to our town. She reportedly planned to build herself a home near her daughter. Staying combat ready is very stressful. I was tired of needing to be armed and vigilant all the time. It was comforting to believe the struggles would soon be over.

The Clerk of Court called to inform me that the executor's bill had been submitted, shortly after construction began on the mother's new home. He asked, if I wanted to see it before he acted on it. His call was a red flag telling me that he saw something he didn't like. Mr. Simmons, the Clerk, was a seasoned politician, with more than 20 years in office. He never made waves himself, preferring to use others for that. I was to be his wave maker this time. Simmons was a true Southern gentleman: loved, respected and definitely someone to stay on good footing with.

The executor hadn't done much that was right from what I had knowledge of. She had spent money as if she wanted to get rid of it; as if her thoughts were, make it go away and the job will be easier. In my opinion, she definitely had not earned the $100,000 she was asking for. The timid and inept performance she turned in had wasted a great deal of money (paying too much for everything and to everyone she had dealings with). I knew without any doubt that I had to challenge her inflated fee.

Legal arguments rely on facts. What facts would help my case to challenge her fee? I needed to locate and organize my evidence into defendable arguments. It came to me that I needed more specific evidence on usual fees, too.

During my meeting with the clerk, he revealed that my objections to the real estate partner settlement had been ignored. The Executor went forward with the building contractor's original contract that I had made a strong objections to several years earlier. I was filled with questions. I greatly resented that she hadn't had the integrity to inform me that she was ignoring my objections. I couldn't abide by a sneaky coward in this situation or in any other.

The clerk's new information lessened my opinion of her and it was already below average. I didn't think that she was a crook until now. I did find her to be overwhelmed, dumb, scared and likely tired of it all, as was I. She could have benefitted greatly by accepting me as her ally. I had shown strong support for her from the start. I told myself, those thoughts and feelings were all in the past now. My loyalties were to my son, as always.

Years later I would learn that she had been charged with knowingly and intentionally misrepresenting a client's legal name to the court while she was also handling Earl's estate. She had to defend her right to practice law in North Carolina according to the court documents posted on line. Perhaps that matter had taken all of her attention to the exclusion of having the time to do our job? If that were the case, then she could have resigned easily enough.

The executor had performed badly in each and every important instance I was aware of. I had to object to her attempt at being excessively rewarded for it and try to recover from her overspending. She became my enemy. I didn't have any emotion about the relationship and that seemed odd at first. I soon accepted the positive affect it fostered.

I decided that whatever resulted next was caused by her own choices. I had a job to do and intended to do it well. My actions linked many people together. If I could free us from having to come back for another karmic round of similar lessons, I wanted to do that.

I awoke early the next morning with a plan to acquire the facts I needed. I went to the local courthouse after considering my options overnight. The Office of Estates and Probate had actual cases, and I could research usual attorney fees paid there. I discovered there had been only one estate in the county that awarded a $100,000 fee to the executor. The estate included several foot traffic businesses that required daily operation; several restaurants and motels, etc. Earl's estate had nothing to require that amount of time and hands on attention. I felt armed to challenge her fee and poor performance.

I was prompted by Earl to hire myself an attorney again. I needed one who was close to the Clerk of Court; he was the decision maker in estates and wills. My insight was confirmed by my psychic connection to the spirit world. It's an interesting relationship working with those in other planes because they know not to override your freewill, unlike some on the earthly plane.

I made it a point to be near the courthouse door during the lunch break for the next few days. My research of estate records gave me the perfect cover to accomplish this without suspicion. The estate office was in front of the door to the parking lot, just where I needed it to be to see which attorney spent the most time with the clerk. I have wondered more than once why I wasn't told to go see "so and so" and hire them to handle the matter, but I wasn't. I was playing my best hand as well as I could see it. Our guides and teachers in spirit don't want to live our lives for us. They can help us with different perspectives and greater insights and direction. Our Free Will is always our own. We are in charge of our actions.

Spirit brings clear and exact guidance forming a strong connection to that energy, making it possible to pass the information on with confidence. It helps to be specific when asking Spirit for assistance. I find it humorous when a person says a psychic was kind of vague. Most often it is coming from a person who dislikes making decisions.

I was able to observe that the usual attorneys and the clerk spent their lunch together from the vantage point of the estate office. He rode with several of them most of time. I selected my attorney after carefully considering each one I had seen accompanying the clerk to lunch more than once that week. Zennie Riggs had been a CPA at the bank before going to law school. I knew he could do the math required and that he could create an accurate spread sheet of expenditures.

Generally lawyers don't like math. I believed someone needed to put the whole ugly truth to a spread sheet to fully comprehend the total extent of the situation. Earl had shown himself to us reading a spreadsheet during our séance with the Durham mediums.

Zennie was also known for being frugal, as he had seven children. He could relate to a parents' wishes for their child. Zennie, most importantly, had an inside track with the clerk, the decision maker in whose hands the estate matters ultimately rested.

Zennie didn't flinch when I told him Earl had been making contact with me and was upset about his assets being wasted. He set to work accessing the estate's financial expenditures right away. I will always be grateful that he was able to immediately bring wasteful spending to a halt.

Thanks to him, the checkbook became taboo for the executor. Going forward only the most necessary bills were paid after the clerk reviewed them. The unlicensed, uninsured builder had been off the estate's nipple since I barred him from the property a year earlier while the executor continued to employ him on her and her mother's properties.

Chapter VI: Path to Peace

I am a fairly pleasant person however, I am not known for my patience. I honestly gave a Goliath effort to being patient during these trying years. The experience had me exploring my own depths of consciousness. I prayed and prayed and tried repeatedly, ad nauseam, to allow the process to evolve in its own time. Even though this was so unlike me, I was growing and stretching into a larger version of myself brought on by Earl's passing and the accompanying challenging events described herein.

One day (it seemed sudden at the time), I couldn't take it any longer. Out of patience and exhausted, I snapped out of the restraints I'd accepted. I was pulling weeds along the flower bed beside my driveway and suddenly I yelled out, "Piss on patience...I want progress." The immense sense of relief I felt helped me to conclude it was correct thinking and it was the right time for a change of circumstances. I sensed a change approaching and grew increasingly eager as a psychic urging followed my initial burst of freedom. The sensation was like a horse at the racetrack waiting to run. I was breaking free! Who needs a starter pistol? Just run with it when the time seems right!

I called my trusty, carefully selected, recently hired attorney, Zennie, and asked to meet with him. He was available right then. Once seated in his office, I explained that I was out of patience and something had to happen to wrap up the estate issues with the executor within the week. I stated that I believed I had waited long enough.

Zennie accepted my insight that the clerk had reduced the estate matter to a "cat fight between two women," in his own mind. I explained that the false perspective gave him permission not to do anything to correct the negative actions in my opinion. Southern men know not to get between fighting women. I'm definitely not a Southern woman and I was not waiting and tiptoeing about any longer. The estate was so much more than a cat fight to me...and to Earl.

Zennie agreed to talk with the clerk the next day and get back to me. I was in his office again, two days later. He asked for more time to convince the clerk to act, assuring me that there were no more expenses to be concerned about. The spending had stopped.

My reaction was nothing to be proud of North, South or even in New Jersey for that matter. Hell flew in me and erupted like a burning oil rig. I spewed profanities like an angry sailor might deliver. I yelled angrily that I was not waiting any longer. No excuse would be good enough to make me wait. Adding, that I knew the clerk had a boss somewhere in North Carolina and I intended to find out who it was. I would then tell this person what had transpired and the length of time it had been allowed to persist. I said that I knew the clerk was failing to do his job and that was going to change. I was going to force a change with or without his help because it's the right thing to do.

I have some pity for Zennie, looking back on that day. He was not in an enviable position, caught between his powerful friend, the clerk, and furious me, who seemed to be channeling an angry Earl Collins. I take responsibility for that scene; it was all me. Zennie pleaded with me not to call the State. It didn't slow me down one moment. I was starting the final battle. I believed it would end the series of ongoing struggles I was fed-up with. "Piss on patience…I want progress; full speed ahead" was my new mantra.

Zennie called to summon me to a meeting in the clerk's office a few hours after I spoke with the State Office of Clerks. I learned from a friend working in a county office that my phone call to the state office of clerks had created rumors in local government offices that "some crazy woman had called the State on Mr. Simmons". I am proud to be able to accept the credit for that call. No one needs to be so secure in a public job that they think they can stop doing it without consequences.

In the clerk's office, the assembled parties sat together in a small room that the clerk used for meetings. Mr.

Simmons appeared red faced, his hands trembled with rage. His voice cracked as he spoke in his usual, but less controlled, soft tone. The result was that a hearing was scheduled the following week. We were to review my objections to the executor's expenditures, including her bill for services rendered at the upcoming hearing.

The executor and her attorney were clearly broadsided at that hearing when I produced original documents for actual materials and labor costs that I'd obtained from the unlicensed contractor long before today's hearing. No one asked, ahead of time, if I had any evidence. I didn't see a need to disclose it.

The end result was a repayment to the estate of $100,000 handled discretely along with the sale of the office building to the executor's mother. Just as the earlier meditation had informed me, "it will be over when her mother gets involved." Spirit is always right. No matter how often I learn this truth I still experience a little doubt when the message received doesn't fit my logical insights.

The office building would become the county's tax office in the near future, a deal worked out behind the scenes at the time it was purchased by her mother. The executor received a greatly reduced fee for her work. A new executor/trustee was appointed. I suggested Earl's CPA be appointed. Earl didn't seem to be guiding from Spirit any longer. Gary Lanvermeier was known as a family man and church-goer with strong ties to the community. He has remained a good friend and positive influence on Chris and his family ever since.

The attorney who represented the executor, throughout the years in which the estate ordeal persisted, apologized to me for being involved. He explained that he had no way out of the case once he was her representative in the initial conflict with the alternate challenger. I assured him I had no hard feelings and didn't see that he'd done anything to hurt us. He passed into Spirit a few years ago. Be free and happy, Carl.

Overall, these experiences forced me to discover and apply intelligence, strength, courage and resilience I hadn't recognized in myself. Yes it came at a cost but I wouldn't have done it differently. If it takes a battle to accomplish the ethically right result then engage in battle and hope to do the least amount of damage possible.

Earl's estate ordeal was my dharma. I fought my battles carefully, accepted that I was not alone, refused to surrender, and I grew in every way. One of the many meditations I recalled while writing this story included a message that the cast of characters engaged in the various roles portrayed here had been together many times and in many places over many lifetimes. Each time they replayed the same story of the "haves" taking advantage of one of their own. This time the intended victim had a champion from the "have nots" social strata. By doing my part, I was aware of the opportunity to bring liberation from the perpetually repeating performances of the tired old story. Consider this: it only takes one actor performing a varied role or reciting a different line to change the story and outcome for everyone.

The desired progress in reincarnation scenarios is for characters to learn greater ethical standards and behaviors, thereby creating more positive story lines and scripts in the future. Victims aren't essential to a story but conflict and resolution are.

The opportunity to rescue one's self and others is available. We need only welcome and claim it.

Epilogue

I continue to apply my psychic-mediumship respectfully and lovingly regardless of the circumstances. My website, www.psychicauthor.com, provides more information on my work. The site is also an easy way to order my self-help products: *Inner Voices* (chakra energy cards), *Speak Stones* (a casting set) and autographed copies of my second book in the Psychic Chronicles Series, There's DNA to Prove It: Message from Beyond, and now this one, too.

Chris grew up, attended college and became a high school teacher. He got married and has two children. His daughter graduated *magna cum laude* from her university in 2014 and is about to graduate from a law enforcement academy. Her goal is to become a detective. Chris's son is in high school and enjoys playing soccer. After nineteen years of teaching in classrooms and coaching a variety of sports, Chris decided to apply to law school. He was awarded an academic scholarship to Liberty Law School, in Lynchburg, Virginia, and has enjoyed the experience immensely.

Chris has applied himself to every opportunity to prepare himself to perform well on either side of assigned cases. He promptly applied his teaching skills to his university life by organizing a study group as soon as he arrived on campus. He will be taking the Virginia bar exam in July 2016. His decision to become an attorney was not influenced so much by his father but rather by friends in his church-circle. One day, I believe he will become a professor of law. Earl will, of course, be attending his graduation ceremony with the rest of the family.

The original executor moved to a larger city with her husband, baby and mother shortly after the estate changed hands. I learned that she decided to retire last year. I wish her peace and wellness. We shared a stressful time that has become part of our past. I know neither of us intended harm to the other.

Most of the people mentioned in this account have transitioned to the world of Spirit. Many of the names used in this story were changed to protect their families. Thirty-two years have passed since we began this challenging adventure. Honestly, none of us had any idea where it would take us. I wish each one peace.

Remember that each person and situation we are aware of is either helping us grow or teaching us an important lesson about life. We are helped in some way by everyone and everything we encounter. Here on earth, we are practicing remembering things we have forgotten. We are becoming better at maintaining balance and emotional equilibrium. Emotions are transitional but thoughts remain until we know enough to choose to change them.

"We learn something from everyone who passes through our lives.
Some lessons are painful, some are painless, and all are priceless."
When we are able to clear our emotions away from the perspectives we experience, lasting truths begin to appear.

I wish every reader peace, clear perspectives, and much love.

About the Author:

Jacqueline Lunger maintains an international spiritual consulting practice. She has amassed a lifetime of unique experiences with non physical intelligences called "Spirits". She shares her real encounters to demonstrate the positive side of loved ones visits and interventions. It is true that love never dies.

She is an ordained minister, certified psychic medium and healer. Throughout her years of service she has been a trustworthy and reliable instrument to those on the other side of life. You are welcome to email for appointments and speaking engagements:

jackielunger@gmail.com.

Jacqueline published her first non fiction book, "There's DNA to Prove It: Message from Beyond" in February 2015. She has created self help tools; Inner Voices chakra energy cards and Speak Stones casting set to help people develop and exercise their own inner senses and abilities.